Homework Helpers

the ancient
EGYPTIANS

by Anita Ganeri
Consultant: Dr. Anne Millard

How to use this book

Each topic in this book is clearly labelled and contains all these components:

Topic heading

Introduction to the topic

Sub topic 1 offers complete information about one aspect of the topic

Words in capitals are explained in the Glossary

War and Weapons

Daggers, like these from Tutankhamun's tomb, would have been used in battle.

Although the ancient Egyptians were not particularly war-like, they were quick to fight their enemies in order to expand their empire. Later pharaohs often led military CAMPAIGNS themselves. Before any campaign, the Egyptians called on the gods to protect the army and help them to defeat their enemies. Scribes accompanied the army into battle, keeping a daily war diary.

THE ARMY

At its height, the Egyptian army is estimated to have been made up of 100,000 men. It was well organized and highly disciplined. The line of command led from the pharaoh through to the generals and officers. The army was made of DIVISIONS of 5,000 men (4,000 foot-soldiers and 1,000 charioteers). The divisions were named after gods, such as Amun, Ptah and Ra.

War scenes, such as the one on this chest, were often painted, providing a record of the events that took place on the battlefield.

▶ **Source: Instructions of the scribe Nebmare-nakht for his pupil Wenemdiamun Miriam Lichtheim, ate New Kingdom**

The long chain of command is clear from this letter:

"Come, [let me tell] you the woes of the soldier, and how many are his superiors: the general, the troop commander, the officer who leads, the standard-bearer, the lieutenant, the scribe, the commander of fifty, and the GARRISON-captain."

WEA

Egyptian soldiers fou spears, battle axes, bow arrows and daggers that w from wood and bronze. For protection, they carried wooden leather shields and wore light armo from leather and bronze. In the New K the horse and chariot was introduced, wh big impact on Egyptian warfare.

Egyptian CHARIOTS were pulled by two were just big enough for two soldiers to st soldier drove the chariot while the other a enemy with his bow and arrows or spear. have only been found in the tombs of pha the rich because they were very expensive.

CASE STUDY

The Battle of Megiddo

In 1467 BCE, Pharaoh Tuthmose III led the Egyptian forces of the prince of Kadesh in the Battle of Megiddo army of 10,000 men and stormed the city, which SU

▶ **Source: Inscription from the Amen Temp c. 1460 BCE**

The Battle of Mediddo was recorded by a carved on the walls of the Temple of Karr

"All the princes of all the northern countries are The capture of Megiddo is the 'capture of a thou

24

ISBN 978 1 84898 073 0

This edition published in 2009 by *ticktock* Media Ltd

Printed in China

9 8 7 6 5 4 3 2 1

A CIP catalogue record for this book is available from the British Library.

Copyright © *ticktock* Entertainment Ltd 2005. First published in Great Britain in 2005 by *ticktock* Media Ltd, The Old Sawmill, 103 Goods Station Road, Tunbridge Wells, Kent, TN1 2DP.

Sub topic 2 offers complete information about one aspect of the topic

Some suggested words to use in your project

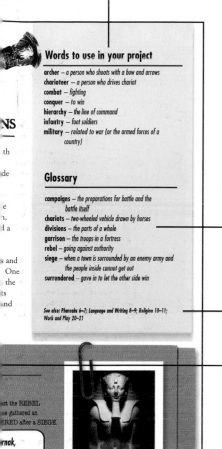

The Glossary explains the meaning of any unusual or difficult words appearing on these two pages

Words to use in your project

archer – a person who shoots with a bow and arrows
charioteer – a person who drives chariot
combat – fighting
conquer – to win
hierarchy – the line of command
infantry – foot soldiers
military – related to war (or the armed forces of a country)

Glossary

campaigns – the preparations for battle and the battle itself
chariots – two-wheeled vehicle drawn by horses
divisions – the parts of a whole
garrison – the troops in a fortress
rebel – going against authority
siege – when a town is surrounded by an enemy army and the people inside cannot get out
surrendered – gave in to let the other side win

See also: Pharaohs 6–7; Language and Writing 8–9; Religion 10–11; Work and Play 20–21

Other pages in the book that relate to what you have read here are listed in this bar

The Case Study is a closer look at a famous person, artefact or building that relates to the topic

Each photo or illustration is described and discussed in its accompanying text

st the REBEL
se gathered an
RED after a SIEGE.

rnak,

nd
hebes:

p within it.
ns."

Pharaoh Tuthmose III's 17 victorious campaigns mean he is remembered as Egypt's greatest warrior-king.

25

Captions clearly explain what is happening in the picture

CONTENTS

The Land of Egypt

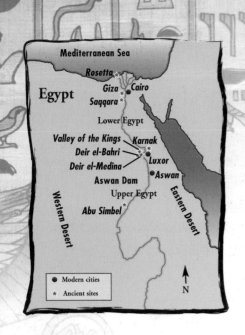

The CIVILIZATION of ancient Egypt was one of the earliest and greatest in the world. It grew up along the banks of the River Nile more than 7,000 years ago, and lasted for more than 3,000 years. The first settlers were probably people who had escaped the droughts of Africa by coming to Egypt.

FIRST DISCOVERIES

For hundreds of years, we knew very little about ancient Egypt. Then, in 1822, a Frenchman named Jean-François Champollion managed to translate the Egyptian system of writing, called HIEROGLYPHICS. Many ancient temples, TOMBS, PYRAMIDS and cities were also explored around this time. Remarkably well preserved by the dry desert heat, the tombs proved to be rich sources of information, as their walls were decorated with scenes of daily life and religious practices. Also, people were often buried with their possessions – including jewellery, furniture, household objects and even clothes and food. These helped experts piece together the details of Egyptian life.

This is a statue of PHARAOH Ramesses II wearing the double crown which symbolized the unity of Upper and Lower Egypt.

We know much about the daily life of ancient Egyptians from tomb paintings, like this one from about 1250 BCE from the Sennedjem tomb in Thebes.

RULED BY KINGS

Over time, the villages of ancient Egypt grew to become towns and cities, and eventually formed two kingdoms – Upper Egypt in the Nile Valley and Lower Egypt in the Nile DELTA. Archaeologists think that King Menes of Upper Egypt united the two kingdoms around 3100 BCE.

▶ **Source: Herodotus, Histories II, c. 480–429 BCE**

The Greek writer Herodotus wrote an account of Egyptian life. His writings tell us that Menes built a new capital at Memphis:

"When this Min [Menes], who first became king, had made into dry land the part which was dammed off, he founded in it that city which is now called Memphis."

Words to use in your project

archaeologists – *people who study history by digging up the past*
artefacts – *ancient objects*
Egyptology – *the study of ancient Egypt*
evidence – *proof*
excavated – *dug up*
mythology – *a set of beliefs*
preserved – *kept intact*

Glossary

BCE – *Before the Common Era*
civilization – *a culture and its people*
delta – *a pile of sediment at the mouth of a river*
hieroglyphics – *the Egyptian system of picture writing*
inexhaustible – *never gets tired*
pharaoh – *an Egyptian king*
pyramids – *triangular-shaped Egyptian tombs*
Ra – *the Egyptian Sun god*
tombs – *where dead bodies are buried*

See also: Pharaohs 6–7; Language and Writing 8–9; Religion 10–11; Farming 18–19; Pyramids and tombs 14–15

CASE STUDY

The River Nile

More than 90 per cent of Egypt is covered in hot, dry desert where very little can grow. Egypt's wealth was based on farming and, without the river, it would not have been successful.

▶ **Source: 'Hymn to the Nile', c. 2000 BCE**

The importance of the Nile is revealed in an ancient poem called 'Hymn to the Nile':

"Hail to thee, O Nile! Who manifests thyself over this land, and comes to give life to Egypt! Watering the orchards – created by RA – to cause all the cattle to live, you give the earth to drink, INEXHAUSTIBLE one."

The River Nile was vital for life to prosper in the deserts of Egypt.

Pharaohs

Ancient Egypt was ruled by kings who were believed to be the god HORUS in human form. The king was given the title of 'pharaoh', which means 'great house', or 'palace'. The pharaoh was head of the government, kept law and order, led the army and controlled trade and industry.

AKHENATEN AND NEFERTITI

Akhenaten ruled ancient Egypt from about 1364–1347 BCE. He was married to Nefertiti.

> ▶ **Source: Amarna letters, 14th century BCE**
> We know a lot about life during Akhenaten's reign from the Amarna letters discovered in 1887. These were letters sent to Akhenaten by officials from the Middle East. One tells how parts of the EMPIRE felt NEGLECTED by the pharaoh:
>
> *"And now your city weeps, and her tears are running, and there is no hope for us. For 20 years we have been sending to our lord, the king of Egypt, but there is not come to us a word, not one …"*
>
> **You can read the Amarna letters at: http://nefertiti.iwebland.com/amarna letters.htm**

A limestone statue of King Akhenaten and Queen Nefertiti.

FEMALE RULERS

There were very few female rulers in ancient Egypt. The most remarkable of these was Queen Hatshepsut, who ruled from 1490–1468 BCE. Sculptures often show Hatshepsut dressed as a man and wearing the CEREMONIAL royal beard. She had a tomb at Deir el-Bahri.

This statue of Hatshepsut stands at her temple in Deir el-Bahri.

> ▶ **Source: Inscription on Hatshepsut's temple at Speos Artemidos, c. 1490 BCE**
>
> Hatshepsut boasted that she restored temples destroyed by foreign invaders:
>
> *"I have raised up what was DISMEMBERED even from the first time when the Asiatics were in the North Land."*

The last pharaoh to ever REIGN in Egypt was Cleopatra VII, who was of Greek DESCENT.

Words to use in your project

correspondence – *letters*
dynasty – *a line of kings*
legacy – *something that is passed on*
monarch – *a ruler*
officials – *people with important duties*
regal – *royal*
successor – *the next person in line to the throne*

Glossary

ceremonial – *used during special ceremonies*
descent – *a person's origin or nationality*
dismembered – *cut or divided up*
empire – *a group of states ruled over by a single king or queen*
Hittites – *ancient people from Anatolia (modern-day Turkey)*
Horus – *the Egyptian god of the sky*
multitudes – *masses*
neglected – *failed to give proper care/attention to something*
reign – *to rule as a king or queen*

See also: Religion 10–11; Pyramids and Tombs 14–15; Priests and Temples 16–17; War and Weapons 24–25

CASE STUDY

Ramesses the Great

Ramesses II (or Ramesses the Great) ruled from about 1279–1213 BCE. During his long reign, he had more temples, statues and monuments built than any other pharaoh. Ramesses also led the Egyptian army in the Battle of Kadesh against the HITTITES.

> ▶ **Source: The Poem of Pentaur, c. 1290 BCE**
>
> Descriptions of Ramesses' army have been found carved on to walls:
>
> *"… [covering] the mountains and the valleys; they were like grasshoppers in their MULTITUDES".*

This statue of Pharaoh Ramesses II stands at Luxor.

Language and Writing

The ancient Egyptians were among the earliest people to create a written language, in about 3500 BCE. Egyptian writing was called HIEROGLYPHICS and each hieroglyph, or picture, stood for an object or idea. The word 'hieroglyph' means 'sacred carving'.

HOW HIEROGLYPHICS WORKED

There were over 700 hieroglyphic signs. Many of these were pictures of people, animals and objects.

Each sign could represent an object or stand for the sound of one or more letters. Hieroglyphs were normally consonants. In order to say a word, vowels had to be added. There were many different ways of writing hieroglyphs – from left to right, right to left or top to bottom.

A statue of a scribe from a tomb in Saqqara.

Hieroglyphs were used for INSCRIPTIONS on temples, tombs and official records. The Egyptians used a much simpler script called HIERATIC for other documents.

The main Egyptian system of writing was called hieroglyphics.

SCRIBES

Hieroglyphs were very complicated. Professional writers, called scribes, had to be trained at special schools. The training began when a boy was nine years old, and took up to 12 years to complete.

Once the students were good enough, they were allowed to write on PAPYRUS scrolls using reed pens dipped in red or black ink. Scribes might work in a temple or for the government.

> ▶ **Source: Papyrus Lansing, late New Kingdom**
>
> One text had this advice for pupils:
>
> *"Apply yourself to this noble profession. You will be advanced by your superiors. Love writing, shun dancing, do not long for the marsh thicket. By day write with your fingers; recite by night. Befriend the scroll … it pleases more than wine."*

Words to use in your project

breakthrough – *a great discovery*
communication – *sharing information*
decipher – *to decode*
documents – *official papers*
palette – *a box containing inks and brushes*
represent – *to stand for*
scholar – *an expert*

Glossary

hieratic – *a simple style of writing used in everyday life*
hieroglyphics – *an ancient Egyptian style of writing using pictures*
inscriptions – *words written on paper, stone or metal*
papyrus – *a paper-like material made from reeds*

See also: The Land of Egypt 4–5; War and Weapons 24–25; Families 28–29

CASE STUDY

The Rosetta Stone

When ancient Egypt was conquered by Rome, the art of reading and writing hieroglyphs gradually died out. Then, in 1799, the Rosetta Stone was discovered – a large stone slab covered in ancient writing. On the stone, the same text was written in three different scripts – hieroglyphic, demotic (a simpler Egyptian script) and Greek. A Frenchman named Jean-François Champollion knew Greek and compared the other two scripts to it. By doing this, he was able to solve the mystery of the hieroglyphs.

The discovery of the Rosetta Stone meant that the ancient Egyptian language could be translated.

Religion

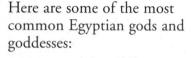

The ancient Egyptians worshipped dozens of gods and goddesses who they believed controlled all aspects of life. Some gods and goddesses were worshipped throughout Egypt. Others were special to particular towns.

Here are some of the most common Egyptian gods and goddesses:

Isis	mother goddess
Ma'at	goddess of truth and justice
Osiris	god of the Underworld
Ra	Sun god
Hathor	goddess of love

THE SUN GOD

The sun god Ra was one of the most important gods in Egypt. He had many different forms and names, and sometimes appears as a man with a hawk's head.

Ra was believed to have created the world and everything in it. According to Egyptian mythology, he sailed across the heavens every morning and through the UNDERWORLD at night.

> ▶ **Source: 'A Hymn of Praise to Ra When He Rises in the Eastern Part of Heaven', Egyptian Book of the Dead, New Kingdom**
>
> The *Egyptian Book of the Dead* contains this description of Ra:
>
> *"The gods rejoice when they see Ra crowned upon his throne, and when his beams flood the world with light … May Ra give glory, and power, and truth speaking."*

This is Horus, the falcon-headed god of the sky.

LIFE AFTER DEATH

The Egyptians believed that after death the soul went to the Next World. But first, the person's soul had to go through a series of trials in the Underworld. If it passed these, it entered the Judgement Hall of Osiris, ruler of the dead.

Souls were tested in the Judgement Hall of Osiris.

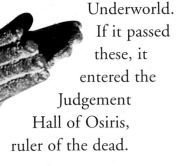

▶ **Source: 'The Negative Confession', Egyptian Book of the Dead, New Kingdom**

If the soul made it to the Judgement Hall, it had to recite the 'Negative Confession', which included the following promises:

"'I have not committed sin ... I have not committed robbery with violence ... I have not stolen ... I have not uttered lies ... I have terrorized none.'"

Words to use in your project

cemetery – *a burial ground*
deity – *a god or goddess*
inscription – *carved words*
judgement – *to be judged by a god*
reincarnation – *being born again*
soul – *the spirit of a person that lives on past death*
spiritual – *religious*

Glossary

avenger – *a person who seeks revenge*
ibises – *large wading birds*
mummified – *the Egyptian way of embalming a body and wrapping it in bandages*
sacred – *having a holy reputation*
sovereign – *a supreme ruler*
Underworld – *the home for the dead according to Egyptian mythology*

CASE STUDY

Sacred Cats

Certain animals such as cats, bulls and IBISES were considered SACRED by the Egyptians. Animals were often MUMMIFIED. An important cat protected the god Ra.

▶ **Source: Inscription on the Royal Tombs at Thebes, New Kingdom**

An inscription on a tomb at Thebes reads:

"Thou art the Great Cat, the AVENGER of the gods, and the judge of words, and the president of the SOVEREIGN chiefs and the governor of the holy Circle; thou art indeed ... the Great Cat."

Many cat statues have been found in tombs dating from around 600 BCE.

Mummies

For a dead person's soul to survive in the Next World, the Egyptians believed that the person's body must be PRESERVED. To stop bodies from decaying, they developed a process called MUMMIFICATION.

HOW MUMMIES WERE MADE

We know about how mummies were made from pictures in tombs and the writings of the Greek historian Herodotus.

> ▶ **Source: Herodotus, Histories II, c. 480–429 BCE**
> This is the process of mummification:
>
> **1.** EMBALMERS washed the body.
>
> **2.** The brain was pulled out through the nose with a hook.
>
> **3.** A slit was cut in the body and the liver, lungs, stomach and intestines were taken out. They were placed in four stone containers called canopic jars.
>
> **4.** The body was cleaned out and packed with natron, salt. Then it was left to dry out for 40 days.
>
> **5.** The body was stuffed with sawdust or cloth, natron and sweet-smelling herbs. The skin was coated with ointment and resin.
>
> **6.** Then it was wrapped in bandages and jewellery.
>
> **7.** Finally, the mummy was placed in a coffin.

A mummy from the Royal Valley, Egypt.

COFFINS

The earliest coffins were plain baskets or wooden boxes. Human-shaped coffins came into use in about 2000 BCE, and stayed in fashion for over 2,000 years. Several coffins might have been placed inside a large stone chest called a SARCOPHAGUS.

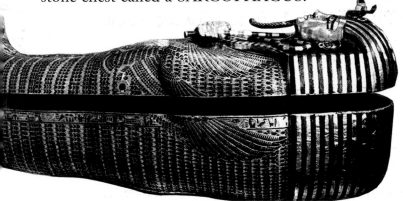

This coffin is made of gold-covered wood, crimson glass and blue pottery.

▶ *Source:* **Egyptian Book of the Dead,** *New Kingdom*
During the MIDDLE KINGDOM, coffins contained spells to protect and guide the dead person to the Next World. One spell read:

"Oh, far strider, I have done no falsehood. Oh, fire embracer, I have not robbed."

Words to use in your project

anthropoid – *human shaped*
corpse – *a dead body*
dessicated – *dried*
excavated – *dug up*
fragrant – *sweet smelling*
ornate – *decorative*
priceless – *very valuable*
purified – *cleaned*
swathed – *wrapped*

Glossary

archaeologist – *a person who digs things up to study history*
embalmers – *people who carried out the mummification*
Middle Kingdom – *the name given to Egypt between 2055–1650* BCE
mummification – *the process of preserving and wrapping a dead body in bandages so that it doesn't rot away*
preserved – *kept for a long time*
sarcophagus – *a stone coffin*

See also: Pharaohs 6–7; Religion 10–11; Pyramids and Tombs 14–15; Priests and Temples 16–17

CASE STUDY

A Famous Mummy

In 1922, the British ARCHAEOLOGIST Howard Carter found the tomb of Pharaoh Tutankhamun in the Valley of the Kings in Egypt. Tutankhamun came to the throne in about 1333 BCE when he was just nine years old and died around age 19. Buried with him was an extraordinary treasure trove.

▶ *Source:* **Howard Carter,** *The Discovery of the Tomb of Tutankhamun, 1922*
The most exciting find of all was described in Carter's diaries as:

"… a magnificent crystalline sandstone sarcophagus intact".
It contained a set of three golden coffins, and in the inner one was the mummified body of Tutankhamun.

This death mask was found on the body of Tutankhamun.

Pyramids and Tombs

To make sure that their bodies were preserved forever, the Egyptian pharaohs had huge TOMBS built for themselves. The first pyramid was built as a tomb for King Djoser in about 2630 BCE. It had stepped sides, but later pyramids were built with flat sides.

HOW TO BUILD A PYRAMID

Historians think that the pyramids were built like this:

1. Teams of builders used wooden sledges to drag stone blocks into position.

2. The blocks were pulled up a ramp made of brick and mud.

Much of what we know about how the pyramids were made comes from EXCAVATIONS.

> ▶ **Source: Herodotus, Histories II, c. 480–429 BCE**
>
> Herodotus described builders at the Great Pyramid of Giza:
>
> *"The stones were QUARRIED in the Arabian mountains and dragged to the Nile. They were carried across the river in boats and then dragged up the slope to the site of the pyramid … They worked in gangs of 100,000 men, each gang for three months. The pyramid itself was 20 years in the making."*
>
> However, despite Herodotus' claims, scholars today believe that only 20,000 men built the pyramid.

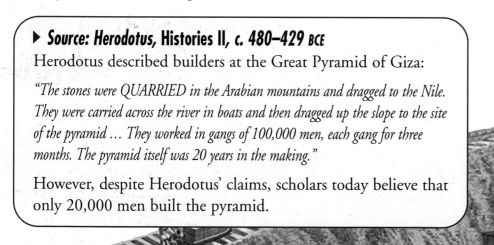

THE VALLEY OF THE KINGS

Many pharaohs were buried in the Valley of the Kings in Thebes.

Later pharaohs chose to be buried in tombs in the Valley of the Kings, a remote valley on the edge of the desert to the west of the city of Thebes. The pharaohs thought that by hiding their tombs in the valley, they would not be targeted by tomb robbers. But both royal and non-royal tombs were filled with treasure and were found by robbers who stole from the tombs across many centuries.

> ▶ **Source: Ali Baba and the 40 Thieves**
> The problem of grave robbers is reflected in the tale *Ali Baba and the 40 Thieves*:
>
> *"… when the chamber was finished, the king stored his money in it … but when opening the chamber a second and a third time, the money was each time seen to be diminished, for the thieves did not slacken in their assaults against it …"*

Words to use in your project

adorned – *decorated*
architect – *a person who designs buildings*
constructed – *built*
implements – *tools*
labour – *work*
looted – *robbed*
majestic – *grand*
monument – *a building that honours a person or event*

Glossary

burial chamber – *a special rooom for a pharaoh's coffin*
excavations – *digging to find ancient buried remains*
quarried – *sourcing precious stones or minerals*
tombs – *places where dead bodies are buried*

See also: Pharaoahs 6–7; Religion 10–11; Mummies 12–13; Priests and Temples 16–17; Trade and Transport 22–23

CASE STUDY

The Great Pyramid

The largest pyramid is the Great Pyramid of Giza. According to the writings of Herodotus, it was built for King Khufu about 4,500 years ago. It stands about 146 metres tall and contains about 3.2 million blocks of limestone, each weighing about 2.5 tonnes. The king's mummified body was buried in a stone sarcophagus in the king's BURIAL CHAMBER, deep inside the pyramid. In the Middle Kingdom, pharaohs had false passages and secret entrances added to put off tomb robbers tempted to steal the treasures buried with the king. Despite these efforts, treasures were still stolen.

The Great Pyramid of Giza was the tallest building in the world for nearly 4,500 years.

> ▶ **Explore the Great Pyramid on the Internet at:** www.pbs.org/wgbh/nova/pyramid/explore/khufu.html

Priests and Temples

Egyptian temples were dedicated to a particular god or goddess and were believed to be their homes on Earth. Only priests and priestesses were allowed to go inside the temples to worship and perform ceremonies. Ordinary Egyptians could only go as far as the temple entrance or the courtyard.

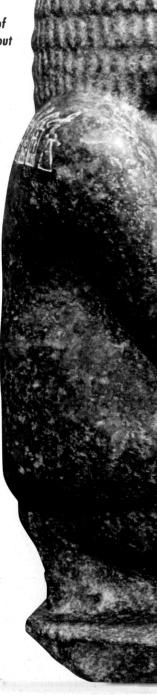

This is a statue of a priest from about 2650 BCE.

TEMPLES

The Egyptians celebrated many annual festivals in honour of the gods and goddesses. On these days, people were allowed inside the temples to celebrate. We know the days the Egyptians celebrated festivals because many calendar dates were inscribed on temple walls.

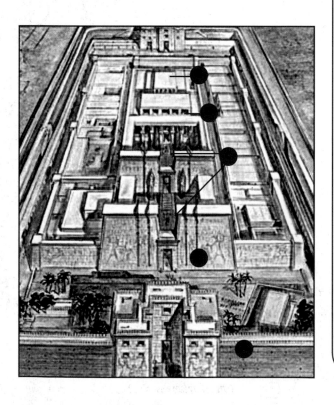

▶ **Source: Temple of Ramesses III at Medinet Habu, c. 1180 BCE**
Studying archaeological remains and art tell us that a typical Egyptian temple followed this form:

• It was surrounded by an outer wall (A) containing a pylon, or temple gateway (B).

• The temple was flanked by two needle-shaped monuments called obelisks.

• Inside were courtyards (C).

• Next came the hall of columns (D).

• At the back was the holy SANCTUARY (E), containing the statue of a god or goddess.

PRIESTS

Each temple had priests attached to it. Besides performing rituals, priests supervised the temple industries, which included brewing beer and tending the temple's lands.

> ▶ **Source: The Ikhernofret Stela, c. 1860 BCE**
>
> A priest described his duties in preparing a body for burial:
>
> *"I DECKED the body of the lord of Abydos with … every costly stone, among the ORNAMENTS of the limbs of a god. I dressed the god in his REGALIA by virtue of my office as master of secret things, and of my duty as priest."*

> ▶ **Source: The Iliad, Book 9, c. 700 BCE**
>
> The writer Homer described how the priests at Thebes were very rich:
>
> *"The heaps of precious INGOTS gleam, the hundred-gated Thebes."*

Words to use in your project

ceremonies – *formal occasions*
festival – *a special day to be celebrated*
performing – *acting*
pious – *very religious*
procession – *a parade*
religious – *believing in a god or gods*
worshipping – *honouring gods*

Glossary

decked – *decorated or dressed*
ingots – *blocks of gold*
ornaments – *decorative objects*
regalia – *objects that symbolize royalty*
sanctuary – *the holiest part of a temple*
sphinxes – *ancient Egyptian stone figures featuring a lion's body and a human head*

See also: Pharaohs 6–7; Religion 10–11; Pyramids and Tombs 14–15; Work and Play 20–21

CASE STUDY

Temple of Luxor

The Temple of Luxor was built by Pharaoh Amenhotep III with later additions built by other pharaohs, such as Ramesses II. The temple was dedicated to the god Amun-Ra and was built in Thebes close to the River Nile. The temple is 259 metres long and 65 metres across. In ancient times a three kilometre-long avenue of SPHINXES connected the temple to the Temple of Karnak.

Line of sphinxes at Luxor

Farming

Many ancient Egyptians worked as farmers along the River Nile. Most people farmed land that belonged to wealthy government officials or temples. Farmers kept part of their crops, but they also had to pay tax to the landowner and the pharaoh. The Egyptian farming year was divided into three seasons.

GROWING AND HARVESTING

Wooden model of a granary with figures from Thebes, Middle Kingdom, about 2000–1800 BCE.

Tomb paintings and small models tell us much about Egyptian farming. In November, farmers ploughed the land and sowed the seeds. In March, the farmers harvested with wood and flint SICKLES. Then, cattle trampled the grain to separate it from the stalks. Next, the grain and HUSKS were separated, and the grain was stored in GRANARIES (see left) until it was required.

> ▶ **Source: Nebmare-nakht, 12th century BCE**
> Farmers worked hard, according to the scribe Nebmare-nakht:
>
> *"By day he cuts his farming tools; by night he twists rope. Even his midday hour he spends on farm labour."*

CROPS

The most common crops in ancient Egypt seem to have been barley and wheat, for making beer and bread. Onions, garlic, lentils, beans, lettuces and grapes were also grown. Egypt's harsh climate had a huge impact on a farmer's YIELD.

Wheat and barley were important crops for Egyptian farmers.

▶ **Source: Hekanakhte and his angry letters, c. 2000 BCE**

In an ancient text, an angry farmer describes the effect of Egypt's climate on crop yield:

"Now, what do you mean by having Sihathor coming to me with old, dried-out northern barley from Memphis, instead of giving me ten sacks of good, new barley?"

Words to use in your project

agriculture – *farming*
deposited – *left*
livestock – *animals*
plots – *pieces of land*
productive – *producing lots of crops*
subsided – *went down, lowered*
tending – *looking after*
unpredictable – *unable to guess*

Glossary

granaries – *buildings used for storing grain*
husks – *the dry outer coverings of fruits and seeds*
inundation – *another word for a flood*
sickles – *sharp hook-shaped tools for cutting grain*
yield – *the extent of crop growth*

See also: The Land of Egypt 4–5; Work and Play 20–21;
Trade and Transport 22–23; At Home 26–27

CASE STUDY

The Flood

The flood season, or INUNDATION, started in July. This was when the River Nile overflowed and flooded its banks, spreading black soil on the fields. While the fields were underwater, work came to a halt. This was the time of year when many farmers were called to help with building royal tombs.

▶ **Source: Herodotus, Histories II, c. 480–429 BCE**

Herodotus recorded the importance of the annual floods:

"It is certain that now they gather in fruits from the earth with less labour than any other men … the river has come up of itself and watered their fields."

Nilometers were built to measure the River Nile during flood seasons.

Work and Play

While most Egyptians worked as farmers and builders, educated men could work as SCRIBES, priests or officials. Craftsmen made everyday items like pots, baskets and sandals. Women were expected to tend to DOMESTIC duties. In their spare time, Egyptians enjoyed music, dancing, wrestling and hunting.

ROYAL TOMB BUILDERS

The men who worked on the royal tombs in the Valley of the Kings lived in a village called Deir el-Medina. The 60 or so workmen were divided into two gangs, each led by a FOREMAN. As well as the workers, men also decorated the inside walls with paintings and hieroglyphs.

▶ **Source: Mortuary stela of Irtysen, New Kingdom**

Ancient documents show how skilled tomb painters were:

"I know how to render the POSTURE of a man's statue, the step of a woman's statue, the wing strength of a dozen birds, the bearing of him who strikes a prisoner, the look an eye casts on someone else and also make fearful the face of the sacrificial victim, the arm of him who hits the hippopotamus, the stance of the runner."

This wall painting from Deir el-Medina shows builders making mud bricks.

GAMES

Egyptian toys included spinning tops, animals on wheels, colourful clay rattles and wooden dolls. Board games were also popular.

Senet was a popular board game that was even enjoyed by the pharaohs.

In a game called senet, players had to try to overcome various dangers to reach the kingdom of OSIRIS. One of the earliest games played in Egypt was called 'the game of snake' because the board was shaped like a coiled serpent. The winner was the first player to reach the snake's head in the centre.

Words to use in your project

appreciated – *enjoyed*
entertainment – *a fun event or activity*
festivities – *celebrations*
income – *wages*
leisure – *free time*
manual – *done by hand*
pastime – *a hobby*
supervised – *watched over*

Glossary

banquets – *lavish meals or parties*
domestic – *relating to the home*
foreman – *a worker in charge of others*
lyres – *musical instruments with strings, like small harps*
Osiris – *the Egyptian god of the dead*
posture – *a way of standing*
scribes – *professional writers*

See also: Language and Writing 8–9; Pyramids and Tombs 14–15; Farming 18–19; Families 28–29

CASE STUDY

MUSIC

Wealthy Egyptians liked to entertain by holding large BANQUETS that included music and dancing. Professional musicians and dancers were hired to entertain the guests. Egyptian musicians played harps, LYRES, cymbals and flutes.

▶ **Source: Coronation inscription of Thutmose III, c. 1500 BCE**
Tomb inscriptions like this one tell us about musical instruments:

"My majesty made a splendid harp wrought with silver, gold, lapis lazuli, malachite and every splendid costly stone."

Music was an important part of Egyptian celebrations.

Trade and Transport

The River Nile was used for travel and to transport goods. The ancient Egyptians even cut a canal through to NUBIA so that they could trade more easily. They also sailed out further to trade with countries around the Mediterranean Sea.

BUYING AND SELLING

Instead of using money, the ancient Egyptians BARTERED goods for other goods that had the same value. Later, a new system was introduced. The value of goods was decided by how many copper weights (or DEBEN) an item was worth. One deben was divided into ten smaller weights called 'kites'.

A painting from the tomb of Panekhmen showing gold rings being weighed out to see how many deben they were worth.

SHIPS AND BOATS

The Egyptians were skilled ship builders. The earliest boats were made from bundles of reeds LASHED together. They were used for travelling short distances on hunting or fishing trips. Later, larger boats were made of wood with oars as well as sails. Many model boats were placed in Egyptian tombs so that the dead person had transport in the Next World. Archaeologists have also found a 40-metre-long barge, built about 4,500 years ago for King Khufu. The DISMANTLED ship was found buried in a pit next to the Great Pyramid at Giza.

Model sailing boats were often placed inside tombs.

See also: The Land of Egypt 4–5; Pyramids and Tombs 14–15; Farming 18–19; At Home 26–27

CASE STUDY

Donkeys

The Egyptians' main way of travelling on land was by donkey. Donkeys were even used for long trading and mining expeditions. However, a donkey cannot survive long without food and water, so travellers had to take plenty with them. All peasants kept donkeys, since farming would have been almost impossible to manage without them. The horse was not introduced to Egypt until about 1650 BCE.

Donkeys were used for transporting the harvest.

War and Weapons

Although the ancient Egyptians were not particularly war-like, they were quick to fight their enemies in order to expand their empire. Later pharaohs often led military CAMPAIGNS themselves. Before any campaign, the Egyptians called on the gods to protect the army and help them to defeat their enemies. Scribes accompanied the army into battle, keeping a daily war diary.

THE ARMY

At its height, the Egyptian army is estimated to have been made up of 100,000 men. It was well organized and highly disciplined. The line of command led from the pharaoh through to the generals and officers. The army was made up of DIVISIONS of 5,000 men (4,000 foot soldiers and 1,000 charioteers). The divisions were named after gods, such as Amun, Ptah and Ra.

War scenes, such as the one on this chest, were often painted, providing a record of the events that took place on the battlefield.

▶ **Source: Instructions of the scribe Nebmare-nakht for his pupil Wenemdiamun Miriam Lichtheim, late New Kingdom**
The long chain of command is clear from this letter:

"Come, [let me tell] you the woes of the soldier, and how many are his superiors: the general, the troop commander, the officer who leads, the standard-bearer, the lieutenant, the scribe, the commander of fifty, and the GARRISON captain."

Daggers, like these from Tutankhamun's tomb, would have been used in battle.

WEAPONS

Egyptian soldiers fought with spears, battle axes, bow and arrows and daggers that were made from wood and bronze. For protection, they carried wooden and leather shields and wore light armour made from leather and bronze. In the New Kingdom, the horse and chariot was introduced, which had a big impact on Egyptian warfare.

Egyptian CHARIOTS were pulled by two horses and were just big enough for two soldiers to stand in. One soldier drove the chariot while the other attacked the enemy with his bow and arrows or spear. Chariots have only been found in the tombs of pharaohs and the rich because they were very expensive.

Words to use in your project

archer – *a person who shoots with a bow and arrows*

charioteer – *a person who drives a chariot*

combat – *fighting*

conquer – *to win*

hierarchy – *the line of command*

infantry – *foot soldiers*

military – *related to war (or the armed forces of a country)*

Glossary

campaigns – *the preparations for battle and the battle itself*

chariots – *two-wheeled vehicles drawn by horses*

divisions – *the parts of a whole*

garrison – *the troops in a fortress*

rebel – *going against authority*

siege – *when a town is surrounded by an enemy army and the people inside cannot get out*

surrendered – *gave in to let the other side win*

See also: Pharaohs 6–7; Language and Writing 8–9; Religion 10–11; Work and Play 20–21

CASE STUDY

The Battle of Megiddo

In 1457 BCE, Pharaoh Tuthmose III led the Egyptian army against the REBEL forces of the prince of Kadesh in the Battle of Megiddo. Thumose gathered an army of 10,000 men and stormed the city, which SURRENDERED after a SIEGE.

> ▶ **Source: Inscription from the Amen temple at Karnak, c. 1460 BCE**
>
> The Battle of Megiddo was recorded by a scribe and carved on the walls of the Temple of Karnak in Thebes:
>
> *"All the princes of all the northern countries are cooped up within it. The capture of Megiddo is the capture of a thousand towns."*

Pharaoh Tuthmose III's 17 victorious campaigns mean he is remembered as Egypt's greatest warrior-king.

At Home

Rich Egyptians enjoyed LUXURIOUS lifestyles, but life was much harder if people were poor. We know much more about how rich Egyptians lived than ordinary people, because the rich left many more objects and buildings behind.

HOUSES

Ancient Egyptian houses were built from bricks made from River Nile mud. Wall paintings tell us that they would have been painted white, with small windows high up to block out the heat and light.

▶ Source: Bill of sale, mid-3rd century BCE

If the land and property were shared, a list of rights like the one below was drawn up to prevent problems:

"You may go up [to] and down [from] the roof on the stairway of this aforesaid house and you may go in and out [of the front hallway by means of the] main doorway … and [you] may make any alteration on it … in proportion to your aforesaid one-eighteenth share …"

Wealthy Egyptians had large houses with shady gardens and pools. Inside, the houses were decorated with FRESCOES on the walls and tiles on the floors. Poor Egyptians had small, simply decorated one-room homes, in which the whole family lived.

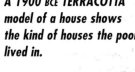

A 1900 BCE TERRACOTTA model of a house shows the kind of houses the poor lived in.

FOOD AND DRINK

The ancient Egyptians ate a variety of foods, including fruits, vegetables, meat, fish, ducks and geese. Poorer people had simple foods, probably consisting of bread, beans, onions and vegetables. Beer was made from loaves of bread broken up and mixed with water. The beer was left to FERMENT and then strained to remove lumps.

The rich frequently held banquets where many courses would be served.

> ▶ **Source: Temple inscription, 2200 BCE**
> One inscription hints at the popularity of beer:
>
> *"The mouth of a perfectly contented man is filled with beer."*

Words to use in your project

banquet – *a feast*
brewing – *making alcohol*
consumption – *eating/drinking*
cookery – *the preparation of food*
delicacy – *a food treat*
interior – *inside*
lavish – *fancy*
trap – *to catch an animal in a device*

Glossary

expedition – *a journey*
ferment – *to turn to alcohol*
frescoes – *paintings done on plaster*
luxurious – *very comfortable and elegant*
terracotta – *brownish-red pottery*

See also: Farming 18–19; Work and Play 20–21; Trade and Transport 22–23;

CASE STUDY

Hunting and Fishing

Tomb paintings show Egyptians hunting and fishing. Small fish were caught in traps, with lines or in nets. Larger fish were caught with spears. Wealthy Egyptians also enjoyed hunting desert animals, such as antelope, hares and foxes, for sport.

> ▶ **Source: Amenhotep III, c. 1415 BCE**
> Even the kings enjoyed hunting, as shown in accounts such as this one from Pharaoh Amenhotep describing a bull-hunting EXPEDITION:
>
> *"There are wild bulls in the desert, in the region of Sheta. His Majesty set out during the night downstream in the royal boat … [killing] a total of 96 wild bulls."*

Fishing and hunting were often enjoyed as sport.

Families

Family life was very important to the ancient Egyptians. The father was head of the family but women had many PRIVILEGES too. Girls as well as boys could inherit their parents' money and property. Children would be adopted if adults could not have any of their own. Old people were greatly respected.

SICKNESS AND HEALTH

Egyptian doctors were well regarded. They may have trained at medical schools, attached to temples.

Doctors worked in the royal court, the community or for the army. By studying the dead bodies of animals, doctors had a good idea of how the body worked.

▶ **Source: The Edwin Smith medical papyrus, probably Old Kingdom in origin**
A doctor's treatment is listed below:

"Diagnosis: One having a wound above his eyebrow. An AILMENT which I will treat.

Treatment: Now after thou hast stitched it, thou shouldst bind fresh meat upon it the first day. If thou findest that the stitching of this wound is loose, thou shouldst … treat it with grease and honey every day until he recovers."

Religion was also important. Doctors recited spells and prayers over their patients.

This temple carving shows a selection of medical instruments.

LOVE AND MARRIAGE

Most marriages were arranged by parents. Girls from poor families might marry as early as 12 years old. Unlike other civilizations of the time, Egyptian men could only have one wife at a time.

> ▶ **Source: Papyrus Lansing, late New Kingdom**
>
> Scribes advised men to treat their wives properly:
>
> *"If you take a wife … she will be attached to you doubly, if her chain is pleasant … If you are wise, love your wife … Fill her stomach, clothe her back … Be not brutal; TACT will influence her better than violence."*
>
> Egyptains could DIVORCE, but most marriages were for life and many couples were buried in the same grave.

Marriage and family were very important in Egyptian life.

Words to use in your project

compose – *to write*
discipline – *to punish*
education – *learning*
legal – *having to do with the law*
matrimony – *marriage*
monogamy – *having only one wife or husband*
symptom – *a sign of a problem*
treatment – *medical care*

Glossary

ailment – *a minor illness*
divorce – *when a marriage breaks down and a couple separates*
memorizing – *learning off by heart*
privileges – *special rights*
tact – *careful handling*
texts – *written works*

See also: Language and Writing 8–9; Religion 10–11; Work and Play 20–21; At Home 26–27

CASE STUDY

School

Most Egyptian children did not go to school. Girls helped their mothers, while boys learned a trade. Some boys went to schools attached to temples. They learned how to read and write by MEMORIZING long TEXTS. Most well-educated boys went on to become scribes.

> ▶ **Source: The Precepts of Ptah-Hotep, 2200 BCE**
>
> If a student did not listen, he might be beaten, as shown in these words of a teacher:
>
> *"But though I beat you with every kind of stick, you do not listen. If I knew another way of doing it, I would do it for you, that you might listen."*

Boys who went to school learned to read and write by copying texts like this one.

Clothes and Jewellery

Ancient Egyptians took a great deal of care over their appearance. Since Egyptian fashion changed very slowly over hundreds of years, people did not have lots of new looks and styles to try out. Instead, they took pride in keeping themselves and their clothes neat and clean. Both men and women liked to wear make-up and jewellery.

CLOTHES

We know what the ancient Egyptians wore from the many illustrations of people in tomb paintings that have survived.

Because of the hot climate, most Egyptian clothes were made of light and loose-fitting LINEN. For men, the basic costume was a practical linen cloth or a simple KILT, wrapped around the waist. Women wore long TUNIC-style dresses. On their feet, people wore simple sandals made from papyrus reeds, although they often went barefoot.

This painting of a middle-class man and woman dressed in finely pleated white linen robes is from a tomb at Deir el-Medina.

JEWELLERY

Rich and poor Egyptians of both sexes liked to wear jewellery. Poorer people wore rings, necklaces and earrings made from cheaper metals, such as copper, decorated with coloured stones and glazes. But wealthy Egyptians had a choice of gold and silver, INLAID with glass or semi-precious stones, such as red carnelian, deep blue lapis lazuli and light blue turquoise.

Wide collars made of many Roman beads were popular throughout Egyptian history.

Egyptian jewellers made necklaces, PENDANTS, bracelets, earrings, anklets and rings. Many pieces of jewellery included sacred symbols, worn as lucky charms. Tutankhamun's tomb contained a magnificent collection of jewellery, revealing the wealth of the pharaohs and the skills of their jewellers.

Words to use in your project

amulet – *a lucky charm*
elaborate – *fancy*
fashionable – *stylish*
pectoral – *a large pendant*
pigments – *colourings*
valuable – *worth a lot*
wealthy – *rich*
weaving – *a way of making cloth*

Glossary

cosmetics – *make-up, perfumes and other beauty products*
inlaid – *decorated with firmly placed objects*
kilt – *short skirt-like garment*
kohl – *a black powder*
linen – *cloth woven from fibres of the flax plant*
ochre – *a type of clay*
pendants – *necklaces*
tunic – *a long sleeveless garment reaching the thighs or knees*

See also: Pyramids and Tombs 14–15; Trade and Transport 22–23; At Home 26–27; Families 28–29

CASE STUDY

Hair and Make-up

Egyptian art tells us that most men and women wore their hair short, which was more comfortable in the warm weather. But on special occasions, such as banquets and official functions, wealthier people liked to wear black wigs made from wool or human hair. Make-up was also widely used. Both men and women used black eye paint, called KOHL, to line their eyes. Lips and cheeks were painted red with powdered OCHRE. COSMETICS were often kept in highly decorated containers. Mirrors were made from polished copper or bronze rather than glass.

Make-up was stored in coloured containers, like these ones found in various tombs.

Index

Ancient Egypt Timeline

About 5000 BCE
Land by River Nile becomes known as Lower Egypt (northern part) and Upper Egypt (southern part).

About 3100 BCE
Lower and Upper Egypt united under one ruler called Menes.

2686–2181 BCE
Old Kingdom.

2680 BCE
Egypt's first pyramid is built at Saqqara.

About 2580 BCE
The Great Pyramid at Giza is completed.

2181–2055 BCE
First Intermediate Period.

2055–1650 BCE
Middle Kingdom.

2055 BCE
Upper and Lower Egypt reunited by Mentuhotep II. The first great temples are built at Karnak.

1650–1550 BCE
Second Intermediate Period. The Hyksos invade from Palestine and nearby, and conquer Lower Egypt.

1550–1069 BCE
New Kingdom.

1,550 BCE
The Hyksos are driven out of Egypt.

1504–1492 BCE
Pharaoh Tuthmose I reigns. First Egyptian ruler to have a rock-cut tomb in the Valley of the Kings.

1352–1336 BCE
Pharaoh Akhenaten rules.

1336–1327 BCE
Tutankhamun is pharaoh.

1279–1213 BCE
Ramesses II rules. Temple at Abu Simbel is built.

1184–1153 BCE
Ramesses III reigns.

1069–747 BCE
Third Intermediate Period.

747–332 BCE
Late Period.

525–404 BCE
Persia invades, taking control of Egypt. After the Persians are defeated, it returns to Egyptian rule.

About 450 BCE
Herodotus visits Egypt.

323 BCE–395 CE
Greek-Roman Period.

343–332 BCE
Persia invades again, regaining control of Egypt.

332 BCE
Persians overthrown by the armies of Alexander the Great. Egypt becomes part of the Greek Empire.

196 BCE
The Rosetta Stone is carved.

51–30 BCE
Cleopatra VII rules. Egypt is conquered by the Romans and becomes part of the Roman Empire.